Ancient Egyptian Sacred Geometry

There are certain geometric shapes that gather and concentrate harmonic and beneficial natural energies of the universe. Some ancient civilizations knew this and knew how to harness these energies. We are now rediscovering these secrets.

Designing Your Home With Sacred Geometry and Other Useful Secrets of Harmonic Resonance
For Greater Peace of Mind, Health, and Well Being

Michael D. Miller

Designing Your Home With Sacred Geometry and Other Useful Secrets of Harmonic Resonance

For Greater Peace of Mind, Health, and Well Being

Background:

Way back in 1976 my dad gave me a book titled "Pyramid Power". He was fascinated with this book. So I read the book. Now, some thirty years later, I can still recall clearly one of the things mentioned in the book: {If a dull razor blade is suspended in a small pyramid that has the same proportional dimensions as the Great Pyramid of Giza, and is suspended one third down from the apex of the pyramid, it will become sharp again. Likewise, if fresh fruit is placed at the same spot, it will never spoil.}

So this improbable bit of information stuck in my mind. But I was never interested enough to pursue the matter further.

Then in 2008 my wife asked me to go to Egypt with her to attend a Rosicrucian tour of the great temples of Egypt. Reluctantly I went. I had little fascination for visiting the Middle East.

The two-week tour changed my life. I experienced some things during the tour that were inexplicable.

First of all, one early morning we visited the temple of Karnack at Luxor. During the tour, I entered a small chamber that contained a 5,000 year-old life-size statue of the Egyptian Goddess Sekhmet. I was totally unprepared for what I experienced. I was overwhelmed by a wonderful feeling of love and happiness. I glanced at the blue-green marble statue at the end of the chamber, wondering what-in-the-heck was happening to me. A picture of this statue is enclosed.

As I stood there for several minutes, the overwhelming energy of love began to overcome me. I panicked and fled the chamber. Later several friends commented to me that I looked "stricken" when I exited the chamber. They were right, although I didn't tell them why.

Then a week or so later we visited the Great Pyramid at Giza. By special invitation we were allowed to enter the King's Chamber. Many tourists visit the Great Pyramid. Thousands daily, actually. From all over the world.

Great Pyramid at Giza

Sekhmet Statue at Karnack

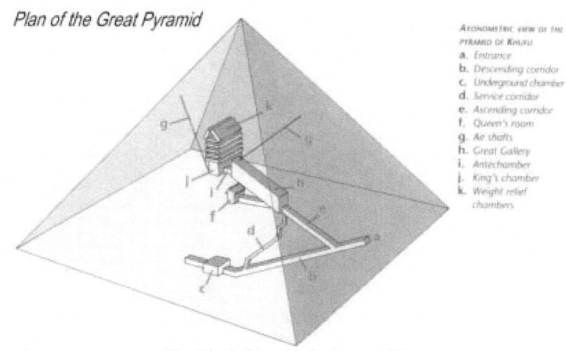

Plan of the Great Pyramid

AXONOMETRIC VIEW OF THE
PYRAMID OF KHUFU

a. Entrance
b. Descending corridor
c. Underground chamber
d. Service corridor
e. Ascending corridor
f. Queen's room
g. Air shafts
h. Great Gallery
i. Antechamber
j. King's chamber
k. Weight relief chambers

The King's Chamber is shown at "j"

The entrance to the King's chamber is via a long, small, tortuous tunnel. So access is of necessity greatly restricted. Thus I felt quite lucky to get to visit this so-sacred place. For you see, the King's Chamber is also located one-third down from the apex of this so-special pyramid. I remembered the information from my 1976 reading of the book "Pyramid Power" that something special occurred at a distance one-third down from the apex of the Great Pyramid.

Difficult Access Tunnel to King's Chamber. Height is 4 ft.

So this time I was expecting to learn or experience something of importance perhaps. I was not disappointed. I had to crawl some 150 feet through the last section of the entrance tunnel that is only about 4 feet high. Then we emerged into a room that was about 18 ft. by 36 ft. in size, with a flat granite ceiling about 24 feet overhead.

This was no place for claustrophobic types. The knowledge that I was standing in a room that was under millions of tons of granite and limestone blocks was a bit overwhelming.

As I stood in the King's Chamber I felt good. The place had a gentle, pleasing presence. The room was bare. No hieroglyphics of any type. All other monuments and temples we visited had been completely covered with hieroglyphics. At one end stood an open red marble box. It resembled on open coffin, and had no lid. It was referred to as a sarcophagus, but I did not believe that is what it was. [A sarcophagus is a stone box into which a king's coffin is placed for safe-keeping].

Some people were crawling into the red stone box to experience what it felt like. I joined the line of people waiting to do this. I crawled into the stone box (it stood about 4 feet high). As I lay back, I was hit with an amazing surge of energy. I wanted to lay there longer, but other people were waiting behind me to have this experience. My best guess is that I was in the box for about 2 minutes.

That two minutes changed my life. During that two minutes I was placed in a position within the red marble box so that all of the tremendous energy created by the perfect symmetry of the millions of tons of marble and granite stone of the perfect pyramid was focused on my heart and aura. Just as a dulled razor blade was perfected by being exposed to the energies of the power spot of a small pyramid, my soul and being was energized by the powers of that special spot in the Great Pyramid.

The pyramid itself possessed its own force centers: the heart of the King's Chamber, its most vital and sacred points, where divine energy was concentrated and especially powerful. The candidate undergoing initiation was placed in the great granite sarcophagus in the King's Chamber at the August moment of the initiation rites (Note: the purpose of Initiation is to bestow upon the disciple certain molecular changes in the body to handle higher energy) because the sarcophagus was in direct alignment with the downpouring ray of cosmic light through the Ark in the Third Eye capstone.

The voltage of such a fiery light ray could only be endured by one in whom the physical, emotional and spiritual forces were completely aligned and purified. The candidate with an unbalanced polarity ran the risk of injury to the physical organism, or even death, because of the accelerated frequencies pouring through the capstone.

From the website http: crystallinks.com/gpac.html

I have since come to believe that Jesus, Socrates, Plato, Napoleon, and all the Pharaohs also lay within that red marble box at one time or another. So I feel very blessed to have had that experience, especially since Jesus is today the most important thing in my life. To have shared that experience with Him is still humbling to me.

My Search Begins:

After I returned from the Egyptian trip, I began to read everything that I could find about Egyptian lore and to get an understanding of what had happened to me. The Internet was a great help. Likewise were a number of books on the subject that are listed in the bibliography.

I discovered that my profound experience in Sekhmet's chamber, and the blissful feeling that I experienced in the King's Chamber of the Great Pyramid, were caused by the perfect symmetry (proportion) of the dimensions of those chambers, as well as their perfect alignment with True North. These perfectly proportioned and aligned rooms had collected beneficial harmonic energies from the planet and the universe, and it was these energies that had affected me so strongly.

The result of my search is this book. Briefly, in a nutshell, what I learned is that there are sacred dimensions that resonate with the creative forces of the universe. The ancient Egyptians knew of this knowledge. They built their temples and municipal buildings according to these rules, using a knowledge of sacred geometry that many believe was brought to them from Atlantis. This sacred geometry was known to ancient civilizations in India, Central and South America, and elsewhere. The Taj Mahal is every bit as much an example of this ancient wisdom as is the Great Pyramid.

What these ancient civilizations knew is that buildings built using the universal laws of sacred design would enhance the physical being of the people who occupied these buildings. Somehow special energies that exist in the universe are drawn to or amplified in these structures so that the overall health, sense of well-being and spiritual balance of those people who inhabit the structures are enhanced.

This sacred design in India has a square central patio

Wikipedia Defines Sacred Geometry: Wikipedia, the Internet dictionary, defines Sacred geometry as follows:

> **Sacred geometry** is geometry used in the design of sacred architecture and sacred art. The basic belief is that geometry and mathematical ratios, harmonics and proportion are also found in music, light, cosmology. This value system is seen as widespread even in prehistory, a cultural universal of the human condition. It is considered foundational to building sacred structures such as temples, mosques, megaliths, monuments and churches; sacred spaces such as altars, temenoi and tabernacles; meeting places such as sacred groves, village greens and holy wells, religious art, iconography and using "divine" proportions.

We, the western societies, experienced this knowledge of Sacred geometry briefly. For when the Templars returned from the crusades in the 13th and 14th centuries they brought this knowledge with them. They had studied at the ancient Egyptian Mystery Schools, and they had access to this knowledge. The most famous cathedrals of Europe were built during this period. Even today we cannot duplicate the mystical and tranquilizing effects experienced by people who stand in the presence of their awesome beauty. It is actually the harmony and perfect proportions of these edifices, not their fancy detail, that cause them to be still so widely visited by thousands of tourists each year. In later centuries, other, more elaborate cathedrals and churches were built, but they lack the power of the edifices built according to the rules of harmony and proportion as taught by the Egyptians. For when the Templars were destroyed in 1307, their knowledge was mostly lost to the world.

Ancient Temples/Cathedrals Built with Sacred Geometry

Angkor Wat in Cambodia; 13th century

Hephaistos Temple in Greece; 300 BC

Chatres Cathedral in France; 1260

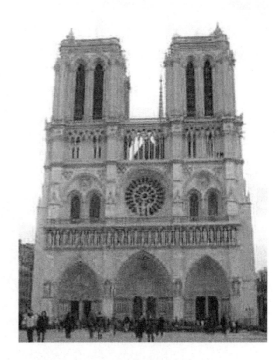

Notre Dame Cathedral in Paris

Cologne Cathedral in Germany; 1248

St. Patrick's Cathedral in Dublin; 127(

Intriguing examples of sacred geometry being used in a discreet and esoteric way up to modern times do exist. So a few did carry on with this knowledge. Shown below is a picture of a simple wooden church that was built in the United States before the Civil War (before 1861). Examination of its floor plan shows that its designer knew and practiced the secrets of sacred design

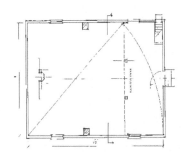

In the above church, the overall length is the square root of two (1.1416) times the width, and the balcony is laid out so that the open area below is a square (1 to 1). The roof pitch is 5:8 (the Golden ratio).

My quest, my search, to better understand what happened to me in Egypt has exposed me to some of this ancient knowledge. The knowledge is still there, but it has to be sought out. I have sought it out, and I now wish to share it with you

One of the first books I encountered was an old copy of the book that I had first read in 1976, entitled "Pyramid Power" by Max Toth and Greg Nielson. It is still good reading. The back cover has these endorsements:

Time Magazine: "Pyramid Power {surrounds} its inhabitants with energy."

Daily News: "The reason for the sustained interest in pyramids is a series of inexplicable and enchanting facts that have been learned about the Egyptian pyramids."

Newsday: "Each basic geometric shape has therapeutic powers, with the pyramid topping the list. Myriad curative powers have been ascribed to pyramids. They....emit psychic energy that causes all sort of miracles!"

The Truth About Mathematics

As I studied about the secrets of sacred geometry, I got a bit peeved about our modern way of teaching mathematics. Mathematics is taught as a boring but necessary subject. Therefore I found math to be tedious, uninteresting, and boring. I "got by" by memorizing what I need to learn. Since I am a Civil engineer, I had to memorize a lot! But as I learned from studying the ancient Egyptian/Atlantean knowledge of math, it is an interesting and vibrant subject.

The Egyptians were the first mathematicians. They taught the western world about math. What Pythagoras, Fibronacci, Socrates and other ancient scholars learned, they got from visiting and studying ancient Egypt. To the Egyptians, mathematics was nothing more than an expression of natural rules of the universe. The rules of mathematics (proportion and harmony) are the same rules used to develop music. Modern architects have referred to architecture as "frozen music". This is because architecture and music are based upon the same harmonic principles of the universe.

What I am attempting to accomplish in this book is to explain how to design a home or improve your life in other manners by utilizing the powers of the sacred geometry of the ancient Egyptians. Living in such a sacred-design home should, according to the many sources referred to in this booklet, expand the happiness, well-being, and health of those that live in the buildings.

The Basics: Floor Plans

Wherever possible, design the building, and its interior rooms to have some of the following floor plan dimension proportions/ratios. The construction should be planned and executed so that said rooms or structure have a finished dimension that is within 1/4 inch of the specified dimension. For example, a room that is planned to be 9 ft. by 18 ft. (a double square) should have a finished interior dimension (from wall to wall) of 9 ft plus-or-minus _ inch by 18 ft. plus-or-minus _ inch. Exact design and strenuous construction discipline will be required to attain this accuracy.

The first basic geometric shapes with mystical power are the circle and the square. The square represents unity. Many ancient structures are built around a square courtyard or atrium. The square has great power.

The second powerful shape is the double square, or a rectangle with the length twice the width. The dimensions of the King's Chamber and the Queen's Chamber of the Great Pyramid, and the dimension of Sekhmet's Chamber at Karnack are all of the double square. Example: the King's Chamber has a floor dimension of 10 cubits by 20 cubits (a cubit = 20.6 inches. The overall dimensions are therefore also expressed as 206 inches by 412 inches).

The third powerful shape is the Golden Ratio, also known as the Golden Triangle. This is simply a rectangle in the ratio of 5:8. The length is a factor of eight, and the width is a factor of five.

Then there are other dimension ratios that can be used for a dynamic floor dimension. They are built around the powers of the square roots of 1 through 5.

The best way to explain these scared design ratios is to use the following graph/drawing. To me, this is the most fascinating and simple and reasonable explanation that I have ever seen for the meanings of the square roots.

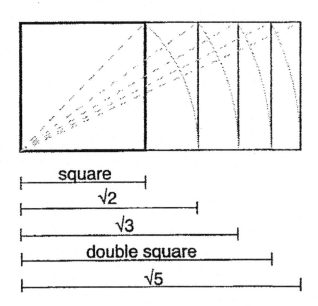

A square, representing unity (1 by 1) is shown.

Next, set a compass point at the bottom left corner of the square. Set the compass length at the length of the diagonal of the square. Swing the compass down to the base line. This makes a length along the bottom line that is equal to the square root of two.

Next set the compass length as the length of the rectangle that is made by the height (1) and the length (square root of two). Swing an arc down to the base line. This length is the square root of three.

In a similar manner we have struck arcs along the base line to show the lengths of the square root of four and five. All of this has been done with a ruler and a compass. No mathematical calculations were required. You could extend this process out further to establish the square root of all whole numbers.

The square root of two is 1.414
The square root of three is 1.732
The square root of four is 2.00 (This is the double square, or 1:2 rectangle)
The square root of five is 2.236

The significance of these numbers is that each of these lengths is also a sacred dimension. For example, a room built in the proportion 1{width}by 1.732 (the square root of three){length} is built according to the principles of sacred geometry.

At this point I must explain that I am only explaining some of the more readily used dimensional ratios of sacred geometry. There are many others that further research will reveal to you. The nature of this book is meant to be simple and concise. But the rules we provide here are amply sufficient to design a fully functional sacred design structure that will harness all of the benevolent energies of the universe.

Summary of Sacred Design Proportions for a floor plan:
To a width expressed as one, a length may be any of the following: 1, 1.414, 1.6 (Golden Ratio), 1.732, 2.00 (double square), 2.236. This is it. Quite simple, actually!

The Fibronacci Series:

The ancient Egyptians used a summation series of numbers that reflect some of the basic design proportions of the universe. To obtain each number of the series, you simply add the two numbers that came before it. In other words, each number of the series is the sum of the two numbers preceding it.

This is not complicated. Lets start with the unity number, one. One plus one is two. Two plus one is three. Three plus two is five. Five plus three is eight. Eight plus five is thirteen. Thirteen plus eight is twenty-one. For practical purposes, I never go any further, but you can (if you wish) carry this summation series out as far as you wish.

What the ancients had discovered is that nature for some reason follows this series as it creates plant and animal life. A well-known example is the nautilus shell, seen below. The beautiful, whirling spiral of the nautilus follows the summation series perfectly.

Many forms observed in nature can be related to geometry (for sound reasons of resource optimization). For example, the chambered nautilus grows at a constant rate and so its shell forms a logarithmic spiral to accommodate that growth without changing shape. Also, honeybees construct hexagonal cells to hold their honey. These and other correspondences are seen by believers in sacred geometry to be further proof of the cosmic significance of geometric forms.

To the left below is a Fibronacci Spiral. This is a geometric spiral whose growth is regulated by the Fibronacci (Egyptian Summation) Series. Its sudden, almost exponential growth parallels the rapid growth of the series itself and mirrors the growth pattern of the nautilus shell.

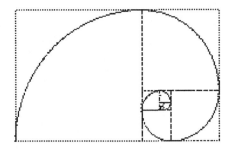

Fibronacci Series replication   Nautilus Shell

There are many other obvious examples. Most flowers and plants develop petals and blossoms and seed patterns that are these summation numbers. Plants and trees develop their branch, stem and leaf formations according to summation series patterns. Leonardo daVinci incorporated the Egyptian Summation Series into many of his most famous paintings and drawings. Even the Mona Lisa has been shown to be drawn according to the summation series.

An Italian mathematician by the name of Leonardo Fibronacci studied in Egypt for many years. He returned to Italy in 1202 and presented the Egyptian Summation Series to the western world. For this reason, this number series is widely known as the Fibronacci Series.

How does this help us? Any two sequential Fibronacci Numbers establish a sacred design ratio. This is especially helpful to me in designing roof or ceiling slopes. I personally usually use a 5 to 8 (Golden ratio), giving the elevation of the slope of the roof a proportion of 5 (rise) to an 8 building width. This is equivalent of a 5 rise to 4 run slope.

Other useful Fibronacci roof/ceiling slopes are:

1:1

1:2

2:3

3:5

8:13

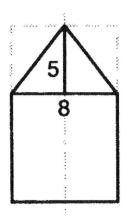

Golden Ratio Roof Slope

Wall Height

We have discussed how to establish the proper width and length of a building or room in order to capture nature's benevolent harmonic forces. Now lets discuss how to establish the proper wall height of your rooms or building.

The standard eight foot interior wall: In the United States the standard interior wall height is 8 ft. Most wood wall studs are cut to make an 8 ft. wall, and the standard length of sheetrock panels is 8 ft. Therefore the easiest wall height to use is 8 ft. If your room width is 8 ft., this is perfect because the ratio of wall height to floor width is 1:1 (a powerful unity proportion). Likewise, we can establish other harmonic proportions that will establish proper floor widths for the standard 8 ft. wall height.

Let us begin with the "square root of two series". The basic square root of two is 1.414. The inverse of this is 1/1.414=.707. These are the two floor width proportions that will be in harmonic resonance with an 8 ft. wall when we use the "square root of two" ratios.

As an example, for the standard eight foot wall, and using the "square root of two" ratios, floor widths that will establish proper harmonics are therefore 8 ft.x1.414=11.312 ft. and also the inverse ratio provides 8 ft.x.707= 5.65 ft. A table is provided below to show possible floor widths using this methodology. I have shown all possible floor widths for the square root ratios for 2, 3, 4 and 5.

Harmonic Floor Widths for an 8 ft. Wall
Using the Square Root Ratios

Number	Square Root or Inverse	Floor Width
2	1.414	11.31 ft.
	.707	5.56 ft.
3	1.732	13.85 ft.
	.577	4.61 ft.
4	2.00	16 ft.
	.500	4 ft.
5	2.236	17.88 ft
	.447	3.58 ft.

Another approach to designing around the standard wall height of 8 ft. is to refer to the Fibronacci Series numbers and their ratios (proportions). Using the Fibronacci Series, we can, for example, use 1:2, 2:3, 3:5, 5:8 and 8:13. A table is provided below to show these floor width possibilities:

Harmonic Floor Widths for an Eight Foot Wall Height
Using the Fibronacci Series

Ratio:	Floor Width
1:2	16 ft.
2:1	4 ft.
2:3	5.32 ft.
3:2	12 ft.
3:5	4.8 ft.
5:3	13.33 ft.
8:13	4.92 ft.
13:8	13 ft.

Some of these possible floor widths as shown in these two charts are impractical (too small), but we are left with the following possible harmonic floor widths for the standard eight foot wall:

8 ft., 11.31 ft., 13.85 ft., 16 ft., 17.88 ft., 12 ft., 13.33 ft., and 13 ft.

The non-standard wall height: Another approach to establishing the proper harmonic wall height is to use a non-standard wall height. This is the method that I prefer to use. Construction costs will be higher, and your building contractor will not like deviating from the standard 8 ft. wall that he has built all of his life. But, for me, the design is more flexible, and I like the effect of taller ceilings.

In this method, you simply use a ratio of 1 (floor width) to either the ratio of the square root ratios or the Fibronacci Series. Or you may use an inverse of these ratios. To illustrate these possible wall heights, I will use an example of a room with a twelve foot floor width.

Harmonic Wall Heights for a Twelve Foot Wide Room, Using Square Root Ratios

Number	Sq. Root or (Inverse)	Wall Height	Comment
2	1.414	16.97 ft.	Too high
	(.707)	8.48 ft.	Good
3	1.732	20.78 ft.	Too high
	(.577)	6.92 ft.	Too low
4	2.00	24 ft.	Too high
	(.500)	6 ft.	Too low
5	2.236	26.83 ft.	Too high
	(.447)	5.36 ft.	Too low

As this chart shows, for a 12 ft. wide room, the only practical harmonic wall height is 8.48 ft. This is a good dimension, as it varies only slightly from the standard wall height of 8 ft.

You can easily prepare similar charts for the floor widths that you will be using in your home or building design.

Another Approach to Wall Height Design: As you ponder on designing your own building, and you consider the possibilities for the proper harmonic wall height, you will realize that your building plans may get a bit complicated if you design a separate wall height for each room of the structure. Construction costs of such a complicated design may soar.

Therefore you may wish to consider a compromise such as the following :

1. Establish which room in your building is the most important from the standpoint of collecting beneficial harmonic energies from the universe. Perhaps this is your main bedroom, or perhaps your living room, or your study.
2. Then design a harmonic wall height for this "main" room. For purposes of discussion lets say that you have designed a "main" room that is 12 ft. wide and has a wall height of 8.48 ft.
3. Then establish 8.48 ft. (which is 8 ft., 5 _ inches) as the standard wall height for your entire building. As you now realize, this means that the other rooms of the house will not have perfect harmonic sacred design proportions. Only the main room will be perfect. You should still design the other rooms with perfectly harmonic floor plans (their lengths and widths should be of harmonic proportions). But they will have a lessened amount of beneficial universal energy because of their imperfect wall heights. My best estimate is that, at the max, you may lose up to 40% of the potential harmonic beneficial energies in these other rooms.
4. This is definitely a tradeoff of function to lower cost. But I like to think that 60% of the beneficial life force energies that will be collected by your less-than-perfect sacred design rooms is still a great improvement of what we design, build and live in now. In other word, 60% is still a great deal! So you will end up with a main room that has 100% collection of harmonic energies, and the other rooms will collect 60% or more. This, in my opinion, is not bad!

A Fascinating Possibility:

There is an intriguing fact about the dimensional proportions of the red marble sarcophagus in the King's Chamber and the dimensional proportions of the Ark of the Covenant. They are the same. Quite a coincidence? Not likely. What is likely is that this is a very special and powerful sacred dimensional proportion.

We have already touched on the fact that the red marble sarcophagus has special powers. Much is written about the mystical powers of the Ark of the Covenant. It is known that only specially trained priests could be around the Ark because of it energies that could harm the unprepared. Is it just possible that the sacred geometry built into the Ark of the Covenant could be responsible for its special energies?

The dimensional proportions of both the red sarcophagus and the Ark of the Covenant are 1 (width) to 1 (height) to 1.666 (length). I believe that this proportion will cause emotional cleansing.

What if we built rooms in our house to correspond to this proportion? If we used a standard wall height of 8 ft., the room would be 8 ft. high, 8 ft. wide, and 13.33 ft. long. This could be a small bedroom or study. If we used a 10 ft. high wall, the floor dimensions would be 10 ft. by 16.66 ft. This is a much larger room, clearly suitable for a bedroom or study. A 9 ft. high wall would correspond to a floor plan of 9 ft. by 14.99 ft. This is also a practical size.

I am anxious to put this idea into practice. If you do, please let me know how it turns out.

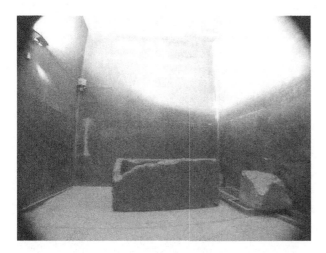
Red Marble Sarcophagus in King's Chamber

Ark of the Covenant

Building and Room Planetary Alignment: All sacred geometrically designed structures are aligned so that their long axis points to True North. This includes the Great Pyramid, Sekhmet's Chamber, all the ancient European cathedrals, and most of the other ancient stone structures of antiquity.

The reason for this is that it is believed that the earth has energy lines that flow between the North and South Poles, and they flow along lines that are parallel to the lines of longitude as shown on topographic maps. By placing the geometrically designed building in alignment with these energy flows, the energies tapped by the sacred design harmonic proportions of the building are maximized.

There is a difference between magnetic north and true north. This difference is caused by the slight tilt of the earth about its axis. The magnetic north spot is always shifting slightly. True North is always a fixed point on the earth.

The difference between true north and magnetic north at any point on the earth is referred to as the Magnetic Declination. A quick review of topographic maps prepared by the US government will show a small chart at the bottom center of the map sheet that shows the magnetic declination for that area. The magnetic declination changes yearly. An experienced map reader or land surveyor should be able to quickly determine for you the magnetic declination for your area. With this information, you can use a magnetic compass to fix the direction of magnetic north, and then plot the directional line of true north.

The best procedure to follow, in my opinion, is to hire an experienced land surveyor to lay out your building with the longitudinal axis pointed directly to True North. I would question the surveyor sufficiently to establish that he knows how to establish true north. I would especially ask him what the magnetic declination between true north and magnetic north at my home site is.

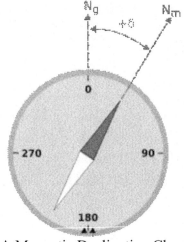

A Magnetic Declination Chart

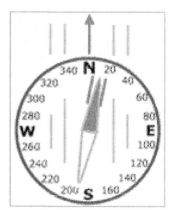

Typical variation between Magnetic North and True North

Sometimes because of the limited size of a building lot, it may not be possible to lay out your building with its longitudinal axis pointed to true north. In this case, if possible, lay out the building so that its width axis points to true north. If this is also not possible, point the longitudinal axis of the building as closely toward true north as is possible. You will experience a slight loss of cosmic energy, but not much.

An Example

Lets sketch out an example of a sacred design building. Shown below is a cottage layout. Please remember that all interior dimensions shown are interior (wall surface-to-wall surface dimensions). The height of all walls is meant to be 8 ft. 5 _ inches. I would probably plan on a 5:8 ratio cathedral type ceiling.

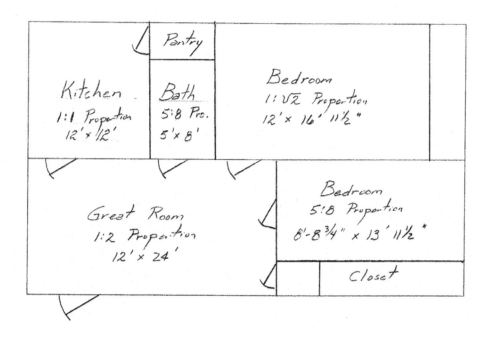

Kitchen
1:1 Proportion
12' x 12'

Bath
5:8 Pro.
5' x 8'

Pantry

Bedroom
1: √2 Proportion
12' x 16' 11½"

Great Room
1:2 Proportion
12' x 24'

Bedroom
5:8 Proportion
8'-8¾" x 13' 11½"

Closet

Sacred Design Floor Plan Sketch for a 960 sq. ft. Cottage

An Explanation of Some of the Mysteries:

According to Plato and Socrates, the continent of Atlantis sank about 10,000 years ago. The sinking of the continent and its surrounding islands took hundreds of years. Therefore there was time for colonies to be sent out to inhabit other areas of the world. Colonies that were set up resulted in the Iroquois nation in North America, The Welsh in Britain, the Basque in Spain, the ruling caste in India, the Jewish race, the Aztec priestly caste in South America, and the ruling caste of Egypt. This is how sacred geometry came to be known in so many diverse parts of the ancient world. This also explains the pyramids that are found in South America, Central America, North America, and elsewhere.

The first pyramid that was built in Egypt was the Great Pyramid at Giza (just outside Cairo). It was built at least 5,000 years ago. All other pyramids were built as copies of this first, magnificent structure, and were built as burial tombs for Pharaohs. The Great Pyramid was not built as a burial tomb; it was built as a religious/spiritual center. Thus there is an absence of hieroglyphics in the Great Pyramid. No one knows the exact purposes for the Great Pyramid. Many believe that the spiritual experience that I had in the red marble sarcophagus of the King's Chamber was one of the spiritual experiences for which the pyramid was built. At a point in his training, each mystery school adept was sent to the King's Chamber to lie in the sarcophagus and have his aura/spiritual being purified, and to connect to the energies of the cosmos. But what else went on in this chamber, as well as the Queen's Chamber and the Subterranean Chamber, is unknown.

It is known that when Napoleon invaded Egypt, he was fascinated by this amazing pyramid. So he spent an entire night alone in the King's Chamber. When he exited the next morning he was visibly shaken. He, for the rest of his life, refused to tell what he had experienced there. On his deathbed, reporters asked him to tell what had happened in the King's Chamber. He hesitated a while, and then slowly said, "If I told you, you would not believe me".

The religious/spiritual endeavors and training schools of the ancient Egyptians are collectively referred to as "The Egyptian Mystery Schools". Many believe, as I do, that Jesus spent time in training there when he was a child. Also it is known that many adepts of the Knights Templar studied there during the crusades of the 11th through 13th centuries. The Great Pyramid is believed to have performed an important part in the mystery schools training.

Most guesses as to how the Great Pyramid was built are wrong. It was not built by sweating, oppressed slaves. It was built joyously by Egyptian farmers during that part of the year when they could not grow crops because of flooding of their fields caused annually by the Nile River. Their gathering together once a year for this undertaking was considered a period of joy and celebration.

Neither were large stone slabs (some up to 20 tons in weight) laboriously hauled up long ramps to build the structure. Proponents of such theories cannot explain where such large stone slabs were quarried, nor can they explain the incredible precision in which the stone slabs were fitted together. Even today, after 5,000 years of weathering, a knife blade cannot be fitted between most if the adjoining limestone blocks. Even today, we could not duplicate such a construction process.

At this point I digress a bit. I lived in Honduras in 1970. I once dug up some ancient Mayan bowls that were made of granite. This was inexplicable since the Mayans did not have metal tools. How did they make these bowls of solid granite? The walls of the bowls were less than _ inch thick. I asked the local natives. They had vague knowledge that their "ancients" knew how to melt stone and thus be able to form it into eating utensils, etc. This, at the time, seemed preposterous. But there was no better explanation.

Then I discovered the stone spheres of Costa Rica. The ancient, perfectly round spheres of granite are, from time-to-time, found in the jungles of Costa Rica. They are up to 6 ft. in diameter and weigh up to 16 tons. They are not located close to any stone quarries, mountains, etc. How did those ancient people construct these spheres? They also had no metal tools. No one knows how they were made. But the idea that they were made, as were the granite bowls of Honduras, by melting the stone so that it could be formed cannot be dismissed.

Ancient Stone Spheres of Costa Rica

On display

As found in the jungle

Now back to Egypt: As I was pondering how the pyramid was built, I met an Egyptologist in Cairo named Leo who was an "out-of-the-box" thinker. He methodically and very logically explained to me that the stone blocks of which the Great Pyramid were built were not hauled into place through superhuman effort and toil. They were cast-in-place.

He said that the ancient Egyptians had a method of melting stone and then recasting it into blocks. He told me that there were a few surviving hieroglyphics that explained this process. However no-one had yet been able to decipher the formula for making the liquefying agent that dissolved the stone. Cyanide was believed to be one of the ingredients. But the other ingredients were not able to be deciphered from the surviving hieroglyphic wall pieces.

As he explained, because each block was cast-in-place, each block fit perfectly up to the adjacent block. Thus the perfect "fit" between blocks. Small pieces of limestone and granite were quarried in far-away mountains, then were easily transported by cart or camel to the construction site. There they were liquefied into a homogenous mass and then poured into wooden forms where they set up into the large limestone or granite blocks that today make up the Great Pyramid.

This explanation is plausible. But what makes it very believable to me is the experiences that I had with the granite bowls in Honduras and the granite stone balls of Costa Rica. Could the same process of melting stone been known to the Maya of Central America and the ancients in Egypt? This is an intriguing possibility.

Architects who design with Sacred Geometry:

I searched the Internet and found an architect in Ireland who designs houses using the principles of sacred geometry. His name is Michael Rice and his website is http://holistichouseplans.com. Shown below are two of his sample houses.

Sacred Design Houses

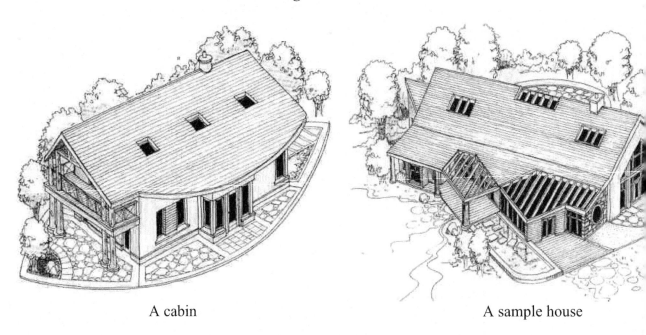

A cabin   A sample house

If you wish to use an architect to design a sacred geometry house for you, you may wish to find a knowledgeable architect such as Michael Rice.

Lets design our own house: Another approach is to design your house yourself. I like this approach. Lets take this approach and design a simple small house or cottage. The floor plan that I developed for this cottage has a main great room (living and dining and family room), two bedrooms, a kitchen, pantry, and one bath. It as has total of 911 sq. ft. of floor space. By starting with such a simple house it will be easier to demonstrate the principles we have been explaining.

Basic Assumptions For the Design:

1. Exterior walls have 2x6 studs (actually 5.5 in. wide), have a _ in. panel of sheathing on the exterior, and have a _ in. panel of sheetrock on the inside wall surface. Any other exterior treatment, such as brick, siding, etc. is considered to be outside of the building layout dimensions. Therefore the exterior wall thickness is _ + 51/2 + _ = 6 _ inches.

2. Interior walls have 2x4 studs (actually 3 _ inches wide), and have _ inch panels of sheetrock on either side. Therefore the interior wall thicknesses are _ + 3 _ + _ = 4 _ inches.

3. The sacred design dimensions of each room are interior dimensions. Therefore when the finished rooms are built, the dimension from each interior wall to the opposite wall must be exactly the sacred design proportional dimensions, to within _ inch. To attain this accuracy, the dimensions of exterior and interior walls will have to be calculated exactly and placed with some precision. To have a precise and attention-to-detail contractor assisting you will be of great help.

4. Our design provides for three of the major rooms to have 12 ft. floor widths. Therefore, as we have explained previously, a wall height of 8.48 ft. (or 8 ft. 5 _ inches) will provide perfect harmonic design proportions for these rooms. However you must also take into consideration the type and thickness of the floor material and the ceiling material. For example, if the ceiling as shown in our cottage design is going to be _ inch wooden boards, then _ inch needs to be added to the wall height. And if a standard hardwood flooring such as _ inch thick oak hardwood strips are to be used as the flooring, this dimension must also be added to the wall height. So, in this case, 1 _ inches would be added to the wall height of 8 ft. 5 _ inches, for a total wall height of 8 ft. 7 _ inches.

5. In our sample house design, we have attained perfect harmonic sacred design proportions in all of the rooms except the bathroom.
   a. Great Room: 12 ft.x 24 ft. (a double square, 1x2 proportion)
   b. Kitchen: 12 ft.x12 ft. (a square, 1x1 proportion)
   c. Main Bedroom: 12 ft.x16 ft., 11 _ inches (the length is the square root of two [1.414] times the width)
   d. Guest Bedroom: 8.725 ft.x13.96 ft (a golden rectangle, 5 to 8 proportion).

6. The bathroom is 5 ft., 3 inches by 8 ft. This is only 3 inches off a perfect 5 to 8 golden rectangle. We could simply add three inches to one of the interior bathroom walls and attain a perfect harmonic dimension here also, in that we would then have a 5 ft. by 8 ft. bathroom interior layout (golden rectangle).

7. For the roof I have chosen the Fibronacci ratio of 1 to 2 for the roof slope. Then by using 2x10 rafters, and having a ceiling material affixed directly to the bottom of the rafters, we also have an interior "cathedral ceiling" with the same 1 to 2 beneficial Fibronacci series slope.

8. Window placement and door placement can vary according to the wishes of the homeowner. This will not affect the sacred dimensions proportions of the house.

9. Likewise the type and thickness of the exterior facing of the house will not affect the interior harmonics. So the use of wider brick, or thinner wooden siding, or whatever, does not affect anything concerning the harmonics of the house. Again,

what is critical is the inside room dimensions that must be kept to the sacred harmonic proportion ratios.

Sacred Design Shadow Boxes

It may not be possible for each of us to live in a home whose rooms resonate to the perfect dimensional proportions of universal sacred geometry. But there is a way in which we can capture some of these beneficial energies for ourselves, cheaply and simply.

Shown below are shadow boxes that I built in my workshop. The first is built using a "double square" dimensional proportion. Its interior dimensions are 3.5 inches by 3.5 inches by 7 inches (the 1:1:2 proportions). I used boards _ inch thick to build this box. I used 1/8 inch plywood for the backing. This box captures energies of joy, happiness, good health and prosperity. I have one of these boxes in every room of my home. In some of the boxes I have added a brass ankh (see second photo) so that I may also capture and amplify into the room the energies captured by the ankh, which are happiness, prosperity and good health. [It is no accident that many hieroglyphs of Pharaohs show them holding an ankh in one hand.] A Christian cross also works well.

Another type of shadow box can be built with the interior dimensional proportions of 1:1:1.666. This is the proportional ratio of the Ark of the Covenant and the red marble sarcophagus in the Kings Chamber. This box generates more serious energies, and should be used with caution. This box will generate healing energies as it projects energies into the room that will lead to cleansing the aura of all negative energies that have accumulated there during ones lifetime. The long-term benefit is of course beneficial, but short term there may be some unpleasantness as the resulting emotional healing takes place.

I placed a double square box with an ankh in the office of my business, and within several weeks my business increased to a significant degree. This happened during a period of economic downturn. This was a nice confirmation for me that the boxes are effective. My wife Debra is shown holding two different shadow boxes.

Shadow Box   **Shadow Box with Ankh (a cross also works well)**

Energizing Water for Better Health and Longevity

Back in the 1980s a man from Arizona by the name of David Hudson discovered (or perhaps "rediscovered") a substance that he named Ormus. He explained that it was the "orbitomically rearranged molecules of rhodium and iridium that exist in the presence of gold".

Some believe that he had rediscovered the material that was referred to as manna in the bible, was known by the ancient Egyptians as Shew Bread, and during the middle ages in Europe was known as the Philosopher's Stone. A detailed explanation of his discovery is beyond the scope of his booklet. But Google has ample coverage of this subject should you wish to explore it further. Laurence Gardner has an excellent book on the subject; ***Lost Secrets of the Sacred Ark: Amazing Revelations of the Incredible Power of Gold.*** Pay special attention to Chapter 11 that explains the David Hudson story. What is important is that many have found that this substance (Ormus) rebuilds youth and extends longevity. They say that it rebuilds a person's DNA, thus renewing youthfulness.

On the Internet you will find a plethora of information about Ormus. Many websites sell Ormus as a powder, and others tell you how to make Ormus water. All of the methods of making Ormus are a bit tedious and/or difficult. But I fortunately stumbled on a way to make the Ormus water simply, using the principles of Egyptian sacred geometry. The story of how I learned this is too long to tell here. Therefore I shall simply tell you how to do it.

The most sacred geometric shape to the ancient Egyptians was the circle. A three dimensional version of the circle is the cylinder. For some reason, if you place a bottle of water within a cylinder, the harmonic forces of the universe will somehow interact to concentrate Ormus energies into the water in the bottle. I don't have a clue as to how this works. It just does. It takes about a week for this process to be complete.

I have learned to speed this process up by using concentric cylinders for my energizing mechanism. Please note the below photo of my energizing device. It takes just 3 days to energize the water with Ormus using my 5 concentric cylinder device. I have five of these 5 concentric cylinder devices so that I have a good and reliable daily supply of Ormus water. I drink 12 to 18 oz. of this water daily.

Further experimentation has shown that three concentric cylinders are sufficient to energize the water in 3 days. I overdid it by making a 5 cylinder device, but then I have a tendency to overdo things!

Ormus Water Concentrating Cylinders

I built my cylinders out of cardboard mailing tubes that I ordered on the Internet. But any material will do. I have used tin cans, plastic pipe, what have you. The material doesn't matter, just the dimensional magic that is created by the cylinder (a three dimensional circle). I used pieces of wine bottle corks as spacers to keep the concentric cylinders equally spaced apart.

If all this seems unbelievable to you, you can easily check it out. Just place two identical plants in pots. Water one with plain tap water, and water the other one with Ormus water. The difference in growth rate and health of the plants will astound you.

Please note the below photo of some two week-old cucumber seedlings. The pot on the left was watered with sacred geometry Egyptian water (stored 3 days in concentric cylinders). The pot on the right was watered with from-the-tap untreated water. This picture speaks 10,000 words.

The Doorway to Enlightenment

Now I am going to wander far astray from sacred geometry (or maybe it isn't that far).

Just before you leave the low entrance tunnel in the Great Pyramid and enter the King's Chamber, there is a symbolic barrier you must conquer. There are three large stone slabs that seem to hang from the ceiling. They are positioned in three keyways that are on each side of the tunnel. They reach down to within 3 ft. of the floor. They appear as a blockage to hamper your progress. In order to enter the King's Chamber, you must bend down low (prostate yourself, so to speak) to crawl under and get past these symbolic barriers.

These three barriers represent the "666" that is widely believed to be the symbol of the devil (Lucifer, the fallen angel). What they really represent is mankind's last great challenge to overcome so that he may find enlightenment. **This last great challenge is mankind's tendency to rely on intellect alone.**

They represent mankind's reliance upon the intellectual mind without the illumination of the spiritual mind. This is perhaps the greatest secret of alchemy, sacred geometry and mankind's spiritual quest.

How simple this truth is. It is so simple that most who read this will not grasp it. "Those that have eyes to see and ears to hear," will understand. So I offer this enticing bit of knowledge to those few who will benefit from it.

When you bend down to pass below the three stone slabs that represent reliance upon intellect alone, you acknowledge to God that you have learned this lesson, and that you know to integrate your spiritual knowledge with the intellectual knowledge from which your material external world is created. Having passed this spiritual challenge, you are then offered the secrets of enlightenment that are contained within the wonders of the King's Chamber, and the amazing spiritual powers of the red stone sarcophagus that rests in the King's Chamber.

What if? Just what if the third dimensional wonders offered by the dimensional sacred geometry powers of the King's Chamber and the red sarcophagus are only third dimensional representations of what also exists within the confines of the un-material world of the spiritual and eternal world of the spirit (the world of God)?

What if you do not have to physically enter the Great Pyramid to experience these spiritual wonders? What if you can know that these spiritual powers that may be experienced in the King's Chamber may be accessed by anybody and at anytime, no matter where you are on the planet? What if you need only state, "I am in the energies of the King's Chamber" to induce the same powerful effects?

What an incredible gift the ancients may have left us. I have been told that the building of the Great Pyramid some five thousand years ago was done as an act of joy on the part of the thousands of farmers and villagers who volunteered to build this magnificent structure. What if their joy was because they knew that they were leaving future mankind a valuable secret that would assist future generations to find spiritual enlightenment? How neat!

And how blessed we are to have discovered these truths. Hooray for you!

Final Author's Comments:

About Jesus and the Egyptians

My sources have indicated that the priests of the Egyptian Mystery School knew all about the birth of Jesus. One of the Three Wise Men was an Egyptian priest. This same

Egyptian priest met Joseph and Mary and guided them to Egypt. Once there, the priests helped hide the family from the Hebrew spies who were frantically scouring the country looking for Jesus. It was easy to hide them in the temples, where access to the Hebrew spies was denied.

When Jesus was three months old, he was consecrated in a ceremony in the King's Chamber. Jesus was laid in the red sarcophagus, resting on a bed of straw so that his heart chakra was at the proper location within the red sarcophagus. Imhotep himself performed this ceremony. Later, when Jesus was five years old, he again entered the red sarcophagus, this time a student of the Mystery School undergoing final initiation.

Bibliography

Note: I have listed the books in the order of importance that I found them to be in writing this booklet.

Pyramid Power by Max Toth and Greg Nielsen; Warner Books Inc., ISBN: not shown

Serpent in the Sky; The High Wisdom of Ancient Egypt by John Anthony West; Quest Books, ISBN: 0-8356-0691-0

Egyptian Harmony, The Visual Music by Moustafa Gadalla; Tehuti Research Foundation, http://egypt-tehuti.org, ISBN 09652509

The Return of Sacred Architecture by Herbert Bangs; Inner Traditions (Bear and Company), ISBN: 1-59477-132-4

Sacred Geometry, Philosophy and Practice by Robert Lawlor; Thames and Hudson, ISBN 0-500-81030-3

Secret Teachings of all Ages by Manly P. Hall, H.S.Crocker Company, Inc. ISBN 978-0-9753-0934-6

Architecture for the Poor by Hassan Fathy; University of Chicago Press, ISBN 0-226-23916-0

Printed in Great Britain
by Amazon

26689344R00020